WRITE TO MARKET

HOW I WRITE A BOOK THAT WILL SELL WELL IN ITS GENRE

SELF-PUBLISHING SUCCESS BOOK TWO

KATE HALL

D1714952

This one is for my Self-Publishing Success gang. If it weren't for you, I wouldn't have started helping people with their journeys.

Introduction

My name is Kate, and I've been a full time author since February of 2020, although I've been publishing books since 2019.

My first book was a complete and utter failure. It sold twenty copies, and I couldn't give paperbacks away. It was a Young Adult Urban Fantasy novel with a cast of queer characters, and it took me five years from the time I started writing it until it was available for sale on Amazon.

I couldn't believe how badly it tanked. I knew this book was going to be what made me successful, and I'd never have to worry about money again.

However, there were about a thousand problems with the book that made it impossible to market, and so I was left scrambling to find any sort of audience in the world of Amazon Self-Publishing.

This is a mistake that thousands of authors make every single year. They write a book that may be great, but it doesn't fit the market they're going for. If you're finding that you have this issue, then don't despair! There's plenty you can do to ensure that your future work reaches the audience you want and makes you some real money.

Disclaimer: This book is for people who want to use publishing to make money. If your goal is just to be able to say that you've published your book, then you might not like what I have to say. Because if you're trying to write for money, then you have to write your books to fit the market. Otherwise, you're cutting your potential sales off at the knees and hurting your chances to succeed.

Now that I've gotten that out of the way, I want to tell you how I personally learned about the "Write to Market" method. I was browsing through the 20Booksto50K® Facebook group, a hub of writers who want to make money from their books. (The goal is to make $50,000 a year from 20 published books).

An author posted about how they wrote their newest book to the market, and it did really well!

Later, I was invited to speak at a writer's conference in Kansas City, Missouri about rapid releasing books. It was still 2019, and despite having several short YA books out at that point, I was still barely making any money. I could talk at length about how to write books quickly (after all, I was finishing a book every week!), but I had no idea how to succeed with said books. The two other panelists, however, announced that they were each making $20,000 per month or more! Meanwhile, I'd barely cleared $50 in a month.

I took the microphone, simply said, "I'm switching genres," and passed it back to the others. The audience laughed, and I definitely said it with some humor. However, I was also serious. I knew that what I was doing wasn't working. People reading self-published young adult fiction weren't picking up what I was writing down.

A month later, I had a cover and an outline for my first Reverse Harem Paranormal Romance novel. Had I written any sort of adult Paranormal Romance to that point? No. Had I been reading it? Also no. However, that didn't matter to me. I knew from other authors that it was entirely possible to succeed with the hungry audience of RH, and I also knew that I was living with my husband at my mom's house.

Once I had a basic outline done, I started my research. I read as much as I could find, and I looked for blog posts and eBooks on the traditional Reverse Harem tropes. I had to succeed, because my life wasn't sustainable.

When I released that book in January, it made $100 in four days. My best month, to that point, had been $88. That was with four YA books and two more adult contemporary books (don't get me started on how badly I messed THOSE up! Just kidding, I'll discuss those more in Chapter X).

In February, I made nearly $700, still from that single book. I was dumbstruck. When book two came out, we were unknowingly about to hit the start of the Covid-19 pandemic, and my husband would soon lose his job, the only thing keeping us afloat. (And even that was barely doing it. Our car was repossessed in March). I was terrified, but March showed me that I wasn't just getting lucky. That month, I made $1750, and then in April, as book 3 came out, nearly $6,000!

I knew that I did my research, and I knew that I was hitting the tropes. I knew that my covers were on point, and I knew that my success was because of all the hard work I put into making my books hit the market tropes. We were able to move out of my mother's house and get a townhouse, and we even bought a car in cash at the end of August!

You may be wondering how you can possibly keep up with market trends, but I'd like to point out right now that trends aren't the point of Writing to Market, and they can change in the blink of an eye. What doesn't change, though, is the expectation that readers build up throughout the genre, no matter what the current trends are.

For example, as I'm writing this, Reverse Harem is having a massive Rejected Mate werewolf boom. If I were to write one of those, it would surely be too late to hit that particular trend. However, if I were to write a werewolf series with the traditional werewolf tropes, then I could succeed at any given time. (Note: Werewolves are a bit of an evergreen creature in paranormal romance. 10/10, would recommend it if you aren't sure where to start).

Now that I've gotten all the introductions and basic definitions out of the way, let's move on to the difference between the unfortunate Write to Market stigmas versus reality.

Best Genres to Write

There are several genres to choose from when you decide to write a novel. You may be starting out with a genre in mind, or, like many others, you might be publishing in order to replace your income but have no idea what's going to actually make you money.

Keep in mind that, in the end, it's entirely your decision what you want to write. If you hate the genre you choose, your journey is going to be far more difficult, and you are more likely to burn out.

I personally have a bit of a tenuous history with genre. I started out writing LGBT+ Young Adult books, all with a paranormal theme. I didn't know anything about the already-existing market behind these types of books, so I wasn't able to hit the market points to sell well. (Even if I did understand the market at the time, I've found that

most LGBT+ books are going to make less money than books with cisgender, heterosexual characters). I didn't find out how low of a seller my genre was until I was invited to speak at a midwestern writers' conference, and my co-panelists were each making around $20,000 per month with their work because they found hot genres and understood the market necessities.

After this conference, I decided to switch gears into writing Reverse Harem romance. I knew plenty of authors who were making ten thousand or more dollars per month doing this, and I knew that it would allow me some of the creative freedom I desperately needed.

When choosing your genre, there are a few things to consider.

1. What's in demand?

If your goal is to sell books, then you need to consider how many people read books in your genre. At the moment I begun to research this book, I decided to check the "Amazon Top 100 eBooks" chart. Out of 100 books, 58 on that chart were specifically a part of the romance genre. 17 more were crime and mystery books, and the rest were divided amongst different categories.

According to a study by BookAdReport.com, Romance and Erotica is worth approximately $1.44 billion per year between eBooks and hard copies. Crime and Mystery, for comparison, is worth $728 million, just over half of that.

Out of the top ten most competitive categories in this study, romance and women's fiction took up six slots, five of those being the top five books. (Many romance books end up categorized under women's fiction on top of other

romance genres, hence why I decided to include it). One of the top selling categories that actually includes crime and thriller is the Women Sleuths category. As far as eBook sales go, readership is overwhelmingly female.

Another massively popular genre is Fantasy and Science Fiction. People like escapism in their literature, and how can you escape the real world better than reading about people in an entirely different world or galaxy?

If you're just starting out, I highly recommend trying your hand at romance. The only real requirements for the genre are, first, that your main characters fall in love, and second, that the story ends in a happily-ever-after (or a happily-for-now, the implication that the characters are leaving the book in love, and readers can interpret the rest of their lives however they wish). Even if your book isn't a romance, it might be worth considering to add a romance subplot to appeal to these readers. (This isn't a requirement, of course, just a suggestion! Many readers hate reading books that have any form of romance, so it just depends on whether you can find that market).

2. Who are your readers?

Even if you don't want to write romance, it's a fair bet that many of your readers will be female, so be sure to consider this when writing. According to a 2016 study by the eBook retailer Kobo, approximately 75% of eBook readers are women, most of which are aged 45 and up. It's theorized that this is related to the ability to change font size and type, making it easier to read. From personal experience, I know that women are more likely to read dozens or even hundreds of books per year. Since joining the Paranormal Romance community, I have met women who read multiple books every day.

Even if you aren't writing books specifically for women, I highly recommend looking into your books to ensure you aren't alienating women, either. Misogynistic writing is falling to the wayside, as the books that end up in the spotlight are the ones with the most readers. IE, women are generally the ones to determine the market. Even in households with children and teens, mothers are more likely to be the ones making book purchasing decisions.

Male readers are also growing less likely to read books that don't consider women during the writing process, as we're seeing a world that's overwhelmingly more aware of the female experience and the ways women have been portrayed in all forms of media for the past century or so.

You might also consider that readership depends on age. According to that same Kobo study, 77% of eBook readers are age 45 and up. I've also found that teens and young adults are more likely to read hard copies, so if your target audience is younger, it may be important to include the option to purchase paperbacks. Since most of my readers are in this 45+ category, I rarely take the time to offer paperbacks, as I only sell a few copies per month.

3. Going against the grain

Another option, of course, is to dismiss all of the previous points. That may sound like a terrible idea, but stay with me for a moment. Do you have specific knowledge of a specific subject? For example, I know a lot about working with silicone for making movie-grade sci-fi prosthetics. If you are knowledgeable about a niche subject that has little information, you could corner the market on that subject!

Just ensure that your books are comprehensive and clear, and you can generally sell them for a bit more than normal eBook publishers. Whilst romance books are everywhere and often have to be priced between $3-$5 to sell well, there aren't very many comprehensive guides on understanding Petrochemical Engineering. Multiple books in this genre sell for $90 USD or more per copy, so even if the readership is low, there's clearly enough demand for experts on that subject that people are willing to pay more.

A good book in a really specific niche can be a great way to make money, but just remember that a smaller market means that, once everyone who wants to has read it, you're unlikely to get new readers. I personally prefer writing books that have a seemingly infinite number of hungry readers, but this other option can work if you're smart about it!

Write to Market
Sereotypes versus Reality

I see it in so many Facebook groups. When someone is begging for information on why their book isn't selling, people ask if it was written to market. I've personally gone into someone's book, reading the blurb and even a few chapters, only to discover exactly why readers don't want that particular piece.

Oftentimes, writers who decide to self publish will create their passion project, knowing for a fact that everyone will want to read it. The cover and tropes don't matter, because this book is perfect!

Hint: It's not. Nowhere close.

When I deign to suggest that the writer consider the market, though, I get angry answers about how writing books to market means selling out, how it means destroying their artistic vision. I see dozens of comments a week about how their book shouldn't have to fit the genre they're writing in order for people to read it. In fact, it's the readers who are wrong!

Another hint: The readers who determine the market are never wrong. I don't care if you hated Twilight when it came out. It was a success because readers wanted it. That's just how the market works. Writers don't determine it, readers do.

If I explain what writing to market really means, and people still argue that it's a bad, evil method, I proceed to roll my eyes and block them. Otherwise, these super angry authors might go in and leave one-star reviews on my books, and they'll say that all my books are garbage because of my methods. It's not worth the hassle, and I don't spend my time on people who only want to complain that their books aren't selling without putting in the critical thought and effort that is needed to succeed.

I could spend a week arguing back and forth, but I would rather educate people who are willing to learn. That's why you have this book open, right? You want to give this Write to Market thing a chance! You are willing to put the work in, because you aren't just someone who complains that nothing works. Like me, you will do everything to ensure your success (by whatever metric you consider to be "successful"), including writing your book to match market expectations.

Here's the reality of Write to Market.

First, it makes writing your books so much easier! If you're baking a chocolate cake, but you've only had one at a birthday party a decade ago, and you don't have a recipe, is it going to be easy? Or would you rather have a recipe and understand what that cake is supposed to taste like? In that same vein, you're going to have a much easier time writing and publishing a book if you understand the recipe you need to succeed.

Second, writing a book to fit the market does not equate to a lack of creativity. Readers have specific expectations of each genre, and if you don't meet these expectations, your books will be skipped and left with bad reviews. However, the same would be true if every book in a genre was exactly the same! There would be no point in reading the same book over and over again, and readers know that each author is going to have a different take on different subjects! Just because you're following the same general tropes (for cozy mystery books, that would be something like "female sleuth moves to a small town and uncovers a crime. Said crime gets solved by the end of the book) doesn't mean that your book isn't your own. Several things like plot, characters, and writing style determine what makes a book unique, not whether or not it fits a market.

That's why authors like Tom Clancy and Robert Ludlum both have plenty of space to publish a thousand action-star books, or why Linsey Hall and CN Crawford can have WILDLY successful Hades and Persephone books that are all published within months of each other! (In fact, these books were part of a coordinated Hades and Persephone trend between authors, and readers read BOTH series as each author promoted themselves and each other!)

There are a few ways you can make your book unique compared to others in the same market.

First, find a new idea for your hero/heroine. What makes them unique compared to others that are selling well? Does this heroine work for the Russian mob before meeting her werewolf boyfriend? Is the hero a retired spy-turned-baker in your contemporary romance? Find something that helps your readers connect to your POV characters!

Second, use details from your own life. Do you know a lot about the Gold Coast in Australia? Did you grow up on a prize-winning racehorse farm? Are you a marine biologist who knows everything about tuna fish? Including details where you have extensive knowledge can really set your story apart from others! This ties into the first point a bit, because if your main character is a specialist in something, people are going to connect to them more easily.

Third, you can add a unique twist on a classic! The cover for Darklight by Bella Forrest is sure to give readers Twilight vibes, but the vampires in this series are like nothing I've ever seen! They're a type of energy vampire from a different dimension, and their skin has patterns of darkness that move around based on their emotions. Sure, it's a book where a human woman falls in love with a male vampire. It hits the expectations like a kiss and admission of feelings in book one, but other than that, it's such a unique story!

Readers want to feel like they're getting a different story every time. These are just a few examples of steps you can take, and there's so much more that can be done. Even if a lot of the world-building details are the same, you will have a unique take on your story! Your "writing voice" is different than everyone else's, to the point that I've seen readers recommend books to an author before finding out that the other books are that same author writing under a pseudonym. Your voice is a big part of what will bring readers to you, and your interpretation of how characters should behave in certain situations will be based on your life experiences.

So long as you're still hitting your main market tropes, readers will be able to connect with your story, and it will be memorable!

Writing to market doesn't have to be a horrible chore. In fact, having an idea of the basic tropes and plot beats you need to include in your story means that you have that much less work to do! You don't have to make everything up as you go, because every successful book before yours becomes a blueprint for your own success. You still have the freedom to interpret these situations however you want, and readers will surely be excited to find yet another voice to their favorite genre.

Research

Now that you understand that Writing to Market isn't something to be afraid of, let's go over how you should start out. Some of these details may seem obvious, but they're important to consider from a Write to Market standpoint.

The first thing you need to do is pick your genre. This is something you should do before you start writing your book, or, if you already have a messy first draft, before you begin developmental revisions. (It can be a lot harder to revise a clean draft, as you probably can't just change the whole plot from this point without tearing your book apart). A genre is going to be how you know what the book needs to look like, in more ways than just the basic plot.

Your genre isn't going to just be a general idea like "romance" or "mystery" that I mentioned earlier, either. Amazon has hundreds of categories where your book might fall, and you want to know exactly what those categories will be before your book is done. This also helps when it comes to picking your keywords later on, as they will determine whether or not people will find your book organically and then buy it.

When you're considering your genre, you want to narrow yourself down. Although your book may fit into several categories, knowing the main ones will help you with your outline and writing process. "Science fiction" isn't what you're looking for here. Is your book a space opera? Is it a dystopian romance? An apocalyptic thriller? You want to be totally aware of what you're writing, or it will make the research stage so much harder.

If you aren't sure what genre you're writing, then this will be a good time to look at similar books on Amazon to what you want to write, then scroll down to their categories. These are the categories of my first book from last year, just as an idea of what you're looking for on the website. You can check these categories with several books, and that will help you narrow down your own genre for the next stage!

Best Sellers Rank: #70,770 in Kindle Store (See Top 100 in Kindle Store)

#2,694 in Fantasy & Futuristic Romance

#3,008 in Werewolf & Shifter Romance

#3,020 in Fantasy Romance (Books)

1. Read in Your Genre

A lot of people get mad when I tell them to take this step, and that's because they don't want to read others. There can be a few reasons for this. First, some authors think that, by reading books similar to what they want to write, they'll end up writing the same thing and come up with something totally unoriginal. Second, there are authors who don't actually enjoy consuming the type of work that they're writing. (I'm going to be honest, I'm not a massive fan of Reverse Harem Romance, but that doesn't mean that I don't sit and read it regularly to keep track of market trends and tropes as they evolve! It's part of my job, and I take it very seriously.)

If you're the first type of author, you should know that, the more you read in this genre, the less likely you are to steal someone else's idea. If you just read one Jack Reacher novel instead of ten Military Thrillers by ten different authors, your book is going to look a lot like a Jack Reacher novel. If you read one Stephen King novel from the eighties instead of ten high-ranking and recent Occult Horror books, your book is going to look like a seventies Stephen King horror novel.

When you read broadly in a genre, you're going to have a good idea of the tropes, and you're going to be less likely to copy anything specific. Reading a ton of books in your chosen genre is also a great way to come up with inspiration. Is there something these heroes do that you find unbelievable or even unreasonable? Here's your chance to change that, to show your own interpretation of these common situations. (Just ensure it doesn't mess up the pacing of the book, like in The Good Place's made-up Six Feet Under: A Chip Driver Mystery Novel written by character Brent Norwalk, where the mystery is solved on page ten. That will just make your readers put the book down and never read your work again).

If you're the second author, then you also might end

up trying to reinvent the wheel if you don't do enough research. By refusing to read books in a genre you plan on writing, you can make some pretty terrible mistakes. I see a lot of this with contemporary romance, where authors will think that they can write it well because they watched The Notebook in 2004. (It's not even contemporary, for one). Or they'll assume that they don't need to read any romance books to understand the genre. You could end up like me, too. In 2019, I wrote a contemporary romance novella with a moderate amount of steamy scenes, but my covers looked like clean romance novels. To say my readers were upset is an understatement, based on the now-unpublished book's two-and-a-half star average reviews on Amazon and Goodreads.

When you depend on old tropes for your "research," you're going to have an outdated book. Tropes shift throughout the years, and by trying to do something original without understanding the genre today, you might actually alienate your potential readers. On the flip side, when you read a lot of vampire books from the past two years, you'll know where the market is currently, and you may even learn to predict where it's going! If you end up popular enough, you might even set a new trend for a few months or more. I know a few self-published authors in Paranormal Romance who help determine the genre's trend shifts, as writers want to emulate their success. These authors are making six figures or more every month, an admirable amount. They are able to achieve this kind of success because they understand the genre!

Reading is just as important as actually writing your

book. As my high school creative writing teacher once said, "To be a better reader, you need to read. To be a better writer, you need to read."

2. Note Taking

When you're reading books in your genre, you don't just want to read through them for entertainment. It takes practice to read books from a writer's eye, so I have some tips on how to do so if you aren't used to it.

1. Make an outline of the plot.

You want to do this for a couple of books. This can be as simple as "beginning, middle, climax, end," or as complicated as writing out the entire sixteen-step three-act structure that I mentioned in A Book A Week. I originally learned to do this when I was in film school by watching Star Wars: A New Hope. It's okay if you don't do this perfectly, but it will get easier as you practice. At this point, I'm able to outline a full novel in thirty minutes to an hour.

2. Look for tropes that are in a lot of the books you read.

In romance, for example, there are a lot of things that readers swoon over. Fake dating (or, one step up, fake marriage!), "there was only one bed," and hot single dads are a few of these tropes, but you want to make sure that the tropes are relevant to the book you plan on writing. These tropes aren't specific to any subgenre, either! Because single dads were popular in contemporary romance, a lot of paranormal romance readers started demanding paranormal books where the love interest was a single dad! (Although maybe he and his kid are werewolves in this case). These tropes differ for each genre, but the more books you read, the more you'll start seeing these pop up.

3. Make a character profile for the main characters.

This can include the lead character, a love interest (or five if this is RH), and the antagonist. A basic profile where you lay out their personality should be good enough, because no matter how different everyone might seem, there are going to be things that connect readers to these characters, the reason these readers stick around in that genre.

These notes are a great way to get used to evaluating books with a critical eye. Once you've done this a few times, you may even stop writing down the details. So long as you know what you're looking for, it will help you understand more about the books succeeding in your genre.

3. Covers and Blurbs

You should also look at the book covers in your genre with a critical eye. What's similar about the covers in the top one-hundred of each genre? What's different? If you plan on creating your own covers, then notes on your genre are important so you can make sure you hit those cover tropes. If you're hiring a designer, you should be aware of your book's genre. You want to hire a designer who's familiar with your particular genre, otherwise your cover might not fit the market where you're advertising. Because the cover is the first thing readers will see, it's the first thing that they will judge. If they see it and it doesn't seem to match what they want to read, they won't even click it.

Each of the following book covers has similar elements. They're both contemporary romance novels, but they convey completely different tones. They use identical fonts with similar layouts, yet they are clearly going to have different moods when you open them.

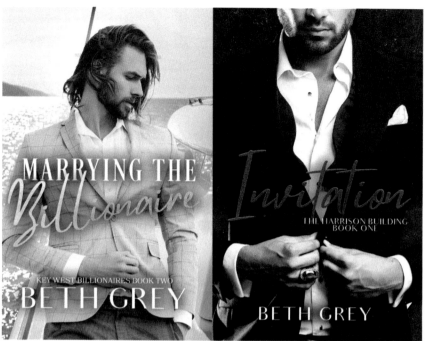

Marrying the Billionaire has a much brighter color scheme, and you can see the man's face. The background is actual scenery, a sailboat on water. Based on this cover, there are certain assumptions that can be made. First, because of the light and airy feel, there probably won't be any steamy scenes. Second, it will be a bit more lighthearted than the other.

On the other hand, Invitation follows some conventions of darker romance. A lot of dark contemporary romance books use deep reds, high contrast, and dark colors. (If you're reading this book in a monochromatic color scheme, such as a paperback or a Kindle Paperwhite, please note that the word "Invitation" is in a deep shade of red, and there's some red splashed behind him in the textured background. The man's skin is the only color on his figure, and that's fairly desaturated).

Whether or not the images are in color should not throw the reader off on discovering the market for either of these books, though. The brightness and contrast, along with the elements on the cover, should be more than enough to tell the genre.

Now, I want you to consider two covers from completely different genres. Can you tell which one is Literary Fiction and which is Paranormal Romance just by glancing at it? What differences make it literary fiction versus paranormal?

This may seem like an obvious example, but it's a quick reminder that a reader will judge your cover with a quick glance. Readers are unlikely to go into your blurb if you decide that the Literary cover is what you want your Paranormal Romance or your Gritty Dystopian to look like. (If you chose the cover with the literal dragons as the Literary Fiction novel, please study a LOT more covers in your chosen genre). The fake cover for Tuscan Hills is brighter, less saturated, and uses a basic sans serif font. However, Dragon Taken has a lot of texture and focuses on a central, magical character. Oftentimes, paranormal covers will have a central color theme to go with the series or other similar elements to tie them all together.

Similarly to needing a fitting cover, you want to make sure your blurb makes your genre clear. When you're looking into the top-selling books in your genre, you should read and evaluate the blurb. Figure out what about it announces its genre (and not the part that says "X book is X genre, that doesn't count). Readers want to know the tone of the book before opening it, and the blurb will give them that idea. A darker book should have a darker description, and vice versa.

I've included samples of two blurbs for my books. The first is from Not My Billionaire, a clean contemporary romance. Although it has some depressing segments, overall the tone is much more casual. It doesn't take itself too seriously, as opposed to a book that has a dark tone overall.

James is not ready to run his parents' multi-billion dollar resort company. Now that they're gone, though, the responsibility falls to him.

Alexis is struggling to make it, but she'll never admit to her family back home that moving to the Florida Keys was a bad idea. The waitressing job isn't too bad, and her apartment only leaks when it rains (which, admittedly, is almost a daily occurrence).

When an accident occurs in the kitchen, James takes the opportunity to learn more about the family business. It most certainly has nothing to do with the cute server who hated him at first sight.

What happens when Alexis finds out who he really is, though? Is their bond enough to keep them together?

Or will the pressure of loving a billionaire be enough to break her?

Next, I've included Rogue Wolf's blurb. Rogue Wolf is about the werewolf mafia, so I used a much more no-nonsense tone for this blurb. The sentences are short and snappy, as the main character is angry with the world and not afraid to show it. These short, concise sentences can be a good way to show anger without including telling the reader how angry the main character is. Combined with the mostly black and white cover, Rogue Wolf is very clearly a dark book with grim themes.

I was alone when my father was murdered.

I was a child when rogue wolves killed him. Then, I was driven out of the pack.
Now, I'm back to claim my rightful place as queen.
I've been training for years to destroy the men who wrecked my life.
Nobody messes with the Lycan pack in St. Louis.
Except me.
I will kill those who tore my family apart, and the rest will get in line.
The wolves will fear me.

4. Reviews

Not only should you read books and study the covers and blurbs, but you should also read reviews for books that you are trying to emulate. Thankfully, this step does not require you to actually read the book. If you're pressed for time, then reading reviews for more books can help you out a lot! (If you're the type of person who can't stand spoilers, you might wait to read reviews until after you've finished the book).

Goodreads and Amazon are both great places to read reviews for other books, although I don't recommend doing it for your own books. Even positive reviews can bring you down, and reviews are mainly meant for readers to determine if they'll like a book, although a book with over-whelmingly negative reviews can be a major red flag.

The best reviews to read are 4-star reviews, as these are generally more positive but unbiased. You're likely to get more out of these reviews, as they also tend to be longer and more detailed in order to explain that rating. If you're looking for details on what to avoid, you can also try checking out some 3-star reviews.

On the flip side, you really want to avoid both 5-star and 1-star reviews.

Although you may want to look at 5-star reviews to find out what readers like about a book, most of them look like this review for Dragon Taken, the first book in my adult Reverse Harem Paranormal Romance series. There's no explanation, no detail. While I, as the author, can appreciate this review, it isn't helpful when you're working on making sure your book is up to snuff. "Awesome!" is not enough detail for you to understand how you should market your book.

☆☆☆☆☆ **Awesome**
Reviewed in the United States on March 29, 2020
Verified Purchase
This book is so flipping amazing! I can't wait to see what's in store for this entire series!

1-Star reviews are just as bad, though! There will always be people who hate your books, and you need to be okay with that. 1-star reviews are going to be where you find these types of people, and even more people who just leave 1-star on everything they ever read. (That's not always the case, but I've found that a lot of the people willing to 1-star a book without regard to the author are going to be impossible to please). This is another review for Dragon Taken, and the things the reader hated are staples of the Reverse Harem genre! Of course my heroine liked the guys fairly quickly, there are four of them that she needs to be smitten with by the end of the book! (Note: This review doesn't bother me, as it's just a part of being an author, but it's also not a constructive or helpful review. Also, a big section of the book 1 review only applied to later books in the series).

☆☆☆☆☆ **Don't get sucked into this series unless divisive political issues are your jive.**
Reviewed in the United States on May 9, 2020
I thought the writing in Book 1 was poor, jumpy, and a bitt skippy. There were also some huge moments where I was like. You were just semi-kidnapped and now you are in a cabin with 4 strange guys. How come you're falling asleep and not totally wired and jumping off the walls.

This four-star review is the exact type of thing that you should be looking for when using reviews for research. The reader mentions a few issues they had with the book, but not in a mean, bitter manner. They also discuss the things they enjoyed about it, which can be helpful for authors who are willing to sift through reviews!

☆☆☆☆☆ **Great start to the series**
Reviewed in the United States on February 3, 2020
I really enjoyed this book. At first it was a little hard for me to get into it but once Serenity met the other dragons and started to interact with her men it got a lot better. I enjoyed her interactions with the other dragons and getting to learn about them and their powers. The males are each very different and yet they all care about Serenity and show it in their own way. There was a bit of insta lust but it makes sense with what happened and how they are connected. I liked the tidbits you got about the dragons and their culture I want to learn more about this world and its politics along with how the magic works. I hope to see more interactions between serenity and her dragon family along with some of the other side characters. Though that ending is such a cliffhanger I need the next book and I hope certain people get their heads out of their asses and stop

I know a lot of authors who get mad or anxious about four-star reviews, but you need to make sure to take them for what they are—overwhelmingly positive! Most of the time, four-star reviewers will turn into 5-star reviewers for the sequels so long as you don't go totally off the rails of your genre, and this can give you a reader for life!

Finally, this 3-star review is a good example of things that I could have done better in this book. Pacing seemed to be an issue with a few readers, so that's something you'll want to consider when writing your own book and researching other books. If readers don't like how fast-paced a book is, they may not pick up book 2. 3-star reviews will often mean that someone won't continue a series, but they didn't despise it the way that 1 and 2-star reviewers might.

☆☆☆☆☆ **Crazy, Fast Story** 🤪😵😱
Reviewed in the United States on August 14, 2020

First you think WTH is going on with this girl, then her family turns out to be A-Holes, and now she's a Dragon Princess!?! Very fast paced, not enough meat for one to really appreciate the story more. #JustMy2Cents 😂 On to the next! #HappyReading ❤

Overall, when looking at reviews, make sure that you look at them with a critical eye. Just because someone left a scathing 1-star review doesn't mean the book is bad or not worth reading, only that the book didn't meet that reader's expectations. (Or, as I've seen with several Reverse Harem authors, the reader hate-reads the genre just to leave bad reviews, as they know there's no chance of them liking the book). Just because someone else left a 5-star review doesn't mean that you'll get anything out of that review. Use your best judgement when deciding which reviews to trust.

Write to Trend

Now that I've spent this whole book so far telling you to write a book to fit your genre, I want to cut in with a very important thing to consider. This can either be a way to do really well with your book's launch, or it can go horribly wrong.

Remember in chapter one when I talked about the difference between Writing to Market and Writing to Trends?

This is something you want to keep in mind when you're doing your research. If all the books in your genre seem to be following a certain trend that wasn't popular a month or two ago, you want to take note. There are often trends to be found, and while it may seem random, these are heavily coordinated efforts between groups of authors to flood the market from the top down. Easily confused with market expectations, trying to write to a current trend can hurt the initial sales of your book or series. (Later on, however, this trend could come back and make your books marketable once again).

For example, academy books were extremely popular in the paranormal scene back at the end of 2019. Many people made tens of thousands of dollars with their paranormal academy books, be it a high school or college setting. However, when writers who spotted this trend later tried to add to it, they weren't as successful. Why? Because trends, as opposed to the core market tropes, come and go in the blink of an eye.

As of July 2021, though, I've seen a shift back toward academy books in the paranormal romance genre, which means that authors who missed out on the initial trend can now market their books that didn't do so well. I'm already seeing friends with academy books whose sales are being boosted by this resurgence in the trend, as readers are excited to find a complete series they haven't read that fits the trend.

Trends starts with the bigger authors, those who are really famous already, or just incredible at marketing. They'll put out their trend-setting novel, and then the fastest writers who aren't already scheduled out months in advance will throw their hats in the ring. Because readers who are long-time fans of these big authors are now hungry for more of that trend, they'll move on to slightly smaller authors. By the time the slower writers (those who take months to write a novel, for example) come into play, the money pool has dried up, and all of the big authors have moved on to the next thing, which becomes the next trend.

My advice? If you aren't writing at a ridiculous pace and keeping track of the year's upcoming trends, just stay out of the mess. My Reverse Harem dragon series didn't fit any trends at the time, and that series alone made me $40,000 for 2020, and it still makes me a few hundred dollars a month to this day. Trends are capable of making you fast money, but they aren't necessary for success. It takes a lot of work and prowess to understand which trends are working and which ones aren't, so keep an eye out!

1. How to spot trends

If you insist on following these trends, then here's what you need to do. Instead of looking at what's hitting the top of the charts today, you need to see what these big-name authors have coming out when you'll be ready to actually publish your series, be it two months from now or a year.

Trends are different from the market due to how quickly they change, so be careful when attempting to write your book to fit a trend! A good rule of thumb is that, if a lot of people are reading and writing it now, it may be best to avoid that particular trend. (For example, in the spring of 2020, paranormal prison books were all the rage, but it was a trend that fell off quite sharply!)

A few tips on spotting a trend:

1. Trends are specific. Werewolf books set in certain locations, like magical academies or prisons, are trends, whereas werewolves are a general theme in the paranormal market. If something seems overly specific, do more research to find out if it's part of a trend or part of the general market.
2. Trends seem to appear out of nowhere. If it seems like

dozens of authors are suddenly topping the charts with the same keywords (IE, Rejected Mates), then that is a trend. Some trends end up sticking around to become a market on their own, like Billionaire Romance, but that's rarely the case. If you are a new author, and you aren't sure if a trend will stick around, it's worth avoiding that trend for now. Once you've built up a readership, you can come back to it, but for now, stick with something that won't fade quickly.

3. Trends fizzle out quickly. Trends in self-publishing tend to last six months to a year. If you've noticed that something has been around for a while, you should probably go ahead and skip that trend. If you want to join a trend, make sure it's something that hasn't started yet by researching preorders coming up in your genre. A good way to check the timing of trends is to check the release date on several books that are similar. If they all came out within a few months of each other, then it's pretty safe to say that it's a trend. Amazon also allows you to set your search to "Newest Arrivals," and if you hit a certain page (especially a recent page!) where that trend stops existing, then it's a good sign that it's a trend that won't last.

You can definitely succeed if you hit a trend at the right time, but getting in at the wrong time can have devastating effects on your finances. Make sure you're careful about which trends you join, and use your best judgement to determine if it might be worth the investment.

2. How to write to trends successfully

I can't guarantee any results, but from my own personal experience, I've found a couple things that work well when it comes to predicting trends in my market.

1. Use the Newest Arrivals feature on Amazon's search. This feature will pull up the furthest preorders first, which means that books that are coming out in a year or more will be at the very top of your screen (after sponsored posts, of course). If you see a lot of books with a certain trope coming out over that time, it's a good thing to note! I've been seeing a lot of preorders go up for vampire reverse harem romances, so I'm jumping in shortly after everyone else with a vampire romance that I started writing after a trend search. Because these other books aren't going to be out for a while, I have the time to make my series great so it will go up when the popularity really starts to gain some steam.

2. Keep an eye out for popular authors in your genre. If an author is well-known in your genre (especially the self-publishing side), it's worth looking at what books they have up for preorder. I'm aware that trends in traditional paranormal romances between one man and one woman tend to trickle down to reverse harem a month or two later, so I like looking at the big authors in paranormal romance. Because I'm a midlist author (meaning that I make a decent living, but I'm not rich or famous), I can benefit really well from following the trends that top-selling authors are setting.

3. Make sure you have time! This is the most important thing when it comes to writing a book that fits a trend. If it seems like the peak of that trend will arrive before you're able to complete your series, then it's worth waiting until that trend comes back, or not writing the series at all. Your time will be better spent ensuring that you have a book that solidly fits the market rather than trying to hit trends that may disappear well before you're able to finish your own work. Timing is so important with this sort of thing, so if you doubt your ability to hit that trend, then either wait to write it or accept that it may be a year or more before your book is as marketable.

It's a great feeling when your book hits a trend at just the right time, especially when you start getting paid those royalties! However, trends can be difficult to spot and even more difficult to hit at the right time, so be sure that you're using caution when it comes to writing your books to fit a trend. Most of all, make sure your book still fits the general market, not just this trend. It still takes the same amount of research as I outlined in the last chapter, plus some extra work and a higher risk. Writing to fit a trend that hasn't arrived yet is dangerous, but can be quite rewarding if you manage to make it work.

Outlining to Market

I hope you're excited, because we're finally to the point where you get to outline your book! (Or look at your already finished outline/draft with a critical eye). The reason this is so late in the book is because you want to understand your readers' expectations before you put too much work into your story. If you spent three months writing a book that doesn't fit in any particular genre, then the marketability is going to be so much harder. When you understand the expectations of your readers, though, you can avoid all that pain and torment.

I'm going to go ahead and drop my three-act structure here for you to reference throughout this chapter, although a more detailed breakdown is available in A Book A Week:

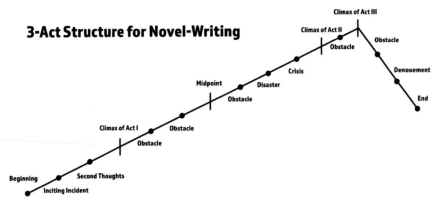

3-Act Structure for Novel-Writing

Climax of Act III

Climax of Act II

Obstacle

Obstacle

Crisis

Denouement

Midpoint

Disaster

End

Obstacle

Climax of Act I

Obstacle

Obstacle

Beginning

Second Thoughts

Inciting Incident

Now that that's out of the way, let's see how you can apply what you've learned to your novel's outline.

First, consider the common Midpoint (aka the turning point) in your genre. In romance, this is often where the main characters kiss for the first time. (Or, for steamier romance, more steamy adult activities). In an action thriller, maybe the hero gets betrayed or beat down. Because I write romance, I generally go with a kiss between my heroine and her love interest. (Or, again, something more for my reverse harem novels). It's also known as the turning point because this is where things take a sharp turn for your characters. It can be a physical shift, like your characters getting injured after a difficult battle, or a mental shift, like a hero deciding to stop ignoring his feelings about his recently-dead spouse.

Next, you want to understand how the climax of your book will go. In a standalone novel, this is where your characters face the antagonist in the final confrontation. This can be an actual villain or just something that's been messing up your character's life. In the first book in a series, you don't want your characters beating the Big Bad quite yet. At this point, they should be facing something less daunting, perhaps a minor villain or a smaller conflict. In my Draecus Clan series, this is where the Hunters and Rebels are introduced, although we don't know anything about their leaders who are sending them to kill the heroine and her mates.

You should also consider how most books in your genre start. It's a big trend right now to start your book with action. From page one, you want your readers to be interested. With things like Kindle Unlimited making it cheaper to read, you want to keep your readers' attention so they don't return it after page one bores them to death. Darklight by Bella Forrest starts with the main character hunting monsters, which draws you right in. What type of monsters are they? How'd they get to an otherwise normal version of our world? How did the heroine get started in this business? My book, Dragon Taken, starts with the main character getting fired from her job and ostracized from her family just before someone tries to murder her.

These are the three most important parts of your novel, so having them solidified is a great way to make sure you're hitting important genre tropes. You can spread the rest of your tropes throughout your book, but these few plot beats will be great to figure out quickly. Having these main points will also help when it comes to outlining and writing the rest of the book, as you've already got an idea of where the story is headed.

At this point, you'll also want to get your character profiles done. Even though your character will be unique in many ways, you want to make sure that they fit the genre's expectations. This is the profile for a romantic lead in one of my upcoming clean romance novels. Something important about him is that he's a genuinely kind man, a trait that clean romance readers are usually looking for.

Leopold (Leo) Patterson

37 • Orlando, Moved from Los Angeles

Role in Story
Love interest of Rebecca.

Goal
To get a promotion back to the position he held at his previous agency.

Physical Description
6'0", stereotypical handsome guy, blue eyes, tan. Chris Pine. Describe Chris Pine.

Personality
Ridiculously friendly. His personality is infectious

Occupation
Digital Marketing Agent, used to be a Digital Marketing Manager before old job fired him for exposing old boss as a predator.

Habits/Mannerisms
Doesn't make a lot of eye contact. When he does, though, it means a LOT. Gets nervous around Becca because she's intimidating and basically a goddess.

Background
He got fired from his previous agency for something ridiculous and had to sign an NDA to keep from getting fired but refused so he could testify in court.

Internal Conflicts
Falling for Rebecca despite knowing he shouldn't get involved with a coworker.

External Conflicts
Rebecca wants the job he wants. He has to go to court because of old boss, who is threatening to blacklist him from the industry. He literally only got the job at Rebecca's agency because their boss was skeeved out by his old boss when she met him at a conference.

Character profiles like this can also help you if you're stuck on the plot of your book, or if you're struggling during the drafting process. Understanding your character and their motivations will make your book: 1) genre appropriate, and 2) interesting.

Even if you don't have all the information you need to fill this out, you'll want to know a few major things. First, the character's role in the story. If you find out that they're unnecessary and just slowing everything down once you're in your editing stage, then you've wasted a lot of time on a character that's just going to get cut from the story. You also want to know their goals. Personally, I like using these goals as a way to torment my characters. Having a goal to throw obstacles in front of is a great way to keep your plot moving. If it's a post-apocalyptic novel, this goal may be as simple as "don't die," and zombies and disease seem drawn to your character like moths to a flame. You also want to know their internal and external conflicts, as this will determine how they react to certain situations. Someone who doesn't believe in love is going to react to a romantic plot far differently than someone who's dreamt of their dream wedding since the day they were born.

When you've finished your outline and understand where your plot is going and how your characters are going to behave, you can move on to the actual drafting process. This is my favorite part of any book (other than designing the cover, but not everyone designs their own covers).

Drafting to Market

When you're drafting your new book, genre expectations are all going to come together, but there are some new things to consider.

Much like writing the blurb, your genre may determine your writing tone. (This will go along with your writing style, something that you'll get accustomed to as you grow as an author).

1. Tone

When I'm writing a darker book, I will often use more formal language. Other than the cursing, of course. However, if it were a dark book for teens, I would tone said cursing down. I also use shorter sentences to help build suspense in certain scenes, which is a common tactic in horror as well. A few short sentences in a row can really bring your audience into the moment, especially if they're on different lines. You don't want to use this all the time, only when you're going for a certain effect.

This scene from Rogue Wolf is just after Eve, my main character, witnesses her father's murder when she's just a child. There are several spots in this chapter where we move into short sentences, including a few one-word paragraphs. Instead of saying "I was panicking," using this type of language shows how her panic makes her drift between her current actions and the reality of her father's death. It also gives a sense of the danger she might be in. She's in a hurry, trying to escape her father's murderer (who isn't chasing her, although she isn't certain of that at this juncture).

Dad is dead.

Dead.

Visions of him assault my mind. That time he let me drive his car in the parking garage, the grin as he brought me a Mcdonald's burger with candles in the top in lieu of a birthday cake, the security of his arms as I cried about mom even though she's been gone for years.

I will never be safe in his arms again.

Because he's gone.

I weave through the evening streets of downtown St. Louis, eventually reaching an Amtrak station.

I hide in the bathroom, my feet up on the toilet seat as sobs burst out of me.

I can't go back there.

Kenneth killed my dad. Thompson's dad is a murderer.

This next excerpt is from one of my older books, a super short contemporary romance. Even though it's in third person, the language is far more casual than that of Rogue Wolf. You get the sense from reading this passage that the main character is tired of her parents' judgement, and that she wants to handle things herself. I consider this to be more of the middle-ground between formal language and casual.

months, though, she's made it much more bright and cheery. A siren sounds off in the distance, and she turns the volume up on the TV. She's not gonna let her parents make her feel bad for dumping Brad. She's just not.

"You guys are welcome to stay with me anytime. I'm only a two hour drive out." In her head, she prays to any god that's listening that they don't take her up on the offer. They usually don't. Mom is allergic to people, and Dad is allergic to the city. That's what they say, anyway.

"Jesus, no," Mom says. Emma lets out a sigh of relief. "We were thinking that you could use a companion. Someone to liven the place up. So you aren't just sitting around watching depressing television all day."

Emma refuses to tell her how accurate she is. It's nearly four, she's still in her pajamas, and a gruesome procedural cop show is on. "I don't need a boyfriend."

Finally, this is the opening of Dragon Taken. I use what I like to consider more of a "realistic" point of view for this series, so my main character is frank and direct, more accurate to how a person might actually think about their situation. This can come across even in narration, and it's very common in the Paranormal Romance genre. Readers of that genre like a heroine they can relate to, and one step toward that is making the heroine's inner voice relatable.

49

I sneer at my phone. I cannot believe that Mom and Dad just bought Adam a condo. A freaking condo!

Meanwhile, I'm still working in the media lab in the basement of a run-down university I hadn't even heard of until I saw the application. The job barely covers rent in my shared three-bedroom, and my bedroom is basically a closet. Well, it is a closet. Converted into a "charming" bedroom. This is not what I needed to find out the day before my rent is due.

It's up to you how you want to write your book, and your style might differ between series as you find your character's voice (or your own narrative voice).

Word choice is important in any genre, and not just the narrative choices. If you're writing a regency romance, your main character isn't going to tell her lover, "Oh, crap, you're right." Even if you aren't writing full-on Jane Austen lingo, you'll want to keep it more formal than you would a contemporary story. A literary novel is going to have a totally different tone than a cozy mystery. This is why your research stage is so important. When you read a lot of books in your genre, you are going to have a much easier time adapting to the tone your book should fit.

2. Good Writing Habits

Aside from tone, you want to consider a few other things in the narrative to ensure your book fits not only its target market, but the publishing industry as a whole. There's a common misconception that self-published books don't have to be well written and that self-published authors don't know how to write, but it's simply not true. If your books aren't written well, people aren't going to read them. This means understanding some pretty basic narrative concepts and applying them in your work.

1. Do you use enough descriptive narration? Your readers want to know what they should be picturing in their heads, and a lack of description can not only make it hard to keep track of things, but also mess up the pacing. Too much description (what I call the Tolkien Method) can also hurt your books by making them too slow. Leave those pages and pages of describing one door for Hobbits.

2. Do your characters speak realistically for their culture? (If the book is in English, this doesn't mean writing down the proper phrases in a different language alongside translation, only that their cadence and word choice works for the story). It's very common for new writers to try to use more formal language when writing dialogue, as that's what we're taught to write for essays and emails in school and the workplace. However, that's not really how humans talk to each other. Instead of saying "Hello, how are you doing today?" a teenager in modern-day America will probably just say, "Hey, what's up?" Skipping contractions ("it is" instead of "it's," "I do not care" instead of "I don't care," etc) is a great way to show readers that you don't know how to write decent dialogue. If you're having trouble, write down some of the things TV characters say to each other in different settings. (The Lannisters in Game of Thrones will talk differently than the Dunphy family in Modern Family).

3. Does your story flow well? Some books have a cliffhanger at the end of every chapter. This works much better for thrillers than it would for a slow-paced lit-

erary piece. There are a few things that will slow down or speed up the pacing in a novel. If it's too fast, then adding sensory description will help, as well as "quiet" scenes that have more to do with character development than the plot's action. On the flip side, if you throw in a long conversation and add a lot of sensory details when your action heroes are supposed to be getting ready to save the president, it will slow down the pacing quite a bit.

4. Will your characters resonate with fans of the genre? Each genre has a different expectation for how characters should be characterized, and this is a great time to refer back to the character profiles you've created whilst outlining. If your character profile fits the genre, and you follow the outline for your character's interactions, then your readers won't have trouble connecting to said character. Just try to make sure they're not one-dimensional stereotypes of genre expectations. Readers want characters with depth, feelings, hopes, and dreams. "The sexy brunette" isn't a character that people will connect with, and they won't care when she's injured. Penelope, the country-girl turned super-spy who's tough on the outside but cries during romantic comedies, however, is someone that your readers would get invested in.

If you follow these steps, it will help you write a better book that will gain more avid readers in your genre. Like I said in the research chapter, the best thing you can do to write well is to read, so look at how other authors are handling their narrative, how they're writing their characters, how they're putting down realistic dialogue. The more you read and practice writing, the better you'll get at creating a story that allows readers to connect.

Conclusion

If you plan to make a full-time living from your writing, it's best to write a book that will fit the market. Hopefully, I've helped you learn a bit about the process.

As a full-time author, I've found the best results the more I hit readers' expectations. When I deviate from expectations, it hurts my sales, and it lowers my readership.

When you move on from this book to work on your own creative journey, there are a few things that I want to make sure you remember and take with you.

First, writing to market is not the same as writing to trends. The market that your book will appeal to is not dependent on fast, temporary trends. The market generally changes over the course of years, not months in the way trends tend to fade. Keep an eye out so you can distinguish the difference between genre expectations and fast-moving trends. If you insist on following trends, just be safe about it. Do your research, and understand that you still may not do as well if that trend flops.

Next, remember to research your genre heavily so that you can give your book the best chance to succeed. A book that's written to market is already leagues ahead of most of the competition, and reading more books in your genre will help you write a better book overall.

Third, keep those expectations in mind when setting up your cover, blurb, and marketing strategy. Your readers won't only judge the interior of the books, but everything they see beforehand. If your cover and blurb don't match their expectations, then they won't even make it to the book you worked so hard on!

As a final note, I know that the task ahead may seem daunting. However, using the blueprint of books in your market will get you that much closer to the finish line. Everyone can succeed, you just need to use the tools at your disposal.

Happy writing!

About the Author

KATE HALL is a small-town writer with a big-city heart. She has two years of college experience and 8 years of running various small businesses. She is also a successful Paranormal Romance author under a different pen name. She lives in Missouri with her husband and their menagerie of pets.

Made in the USA
Middletown, DE
26 November 2022

16093710R00035